Prevailing Prayers of the BIBLE

of the

Kimberly Ray

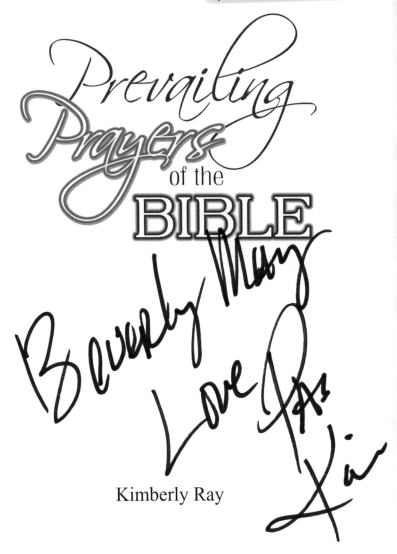

Prevailing Prayers of the BIBLE

Kimberly Ray

All scriptural quotations are from the
King James Version of the Holy Bible

The Prevailing Prayers of the Bible

Published by:
Angie Ray Ministries Storehouse, Inc.
P.O. Box 1104
Matteson, Illinois 60443
ISBN # 978-1-60402-422-7

Book Production by:
Angie Ray Ministries
Matteson, Illinois

Printed in the United States of America

BIBLE

Kimberly Ray

Dedication

To the memory of my compassionate,

consecrated and royal Mother, the late

Dr. Angie Ray, who was responsible for teaching

me to love the Lord with all my heart and the

art of Intercession.

My Experience

At the tender age of 10, I received salvation during a New Years' Eve church service in the city of Chicago. I had an acute awareness of the presence of God as a child and I was drawn to the Lord in an unusual way. There was something intriguing about the ability to pray, the reality that I could talk to the Creator of the world; this Sovereign, Holy, Majestic God and know that He could hear and answer my prayers.

I was blessed to be raised by a God-fearing mother and father. Mom and Dad would call us together to pray.

My mother, Dr. Angie Ray was a loving, decent and honorable woman, who had a remarkable gift to pray and teach others dimensions of prayer. Dr. Ray became a pioneer and trailblazer in the area of prayer, intercession and deliverance. Day after day for countless hours, I personally experienced the power of consistent fervent prayer. People came from far and near, day and night to receive prayer regarding their concerns and needs. I observed Dr. Ray pray with prominent leaders and public officials as well as the body of Christ in general. Rarely did a day go by without hearing the sound of prayer.

There was such a strong sense of reverence and awe as we were instructed to speak our pure hearts to the Lord. During prayer everything else was secondary. We were instructed to wait before God and yield to His Holy Spirit. There were times during prayer, that we would feel the power of God. Often my response would be to weep because of the overwhelming love and presence of God. As we held hands during family prayer and poured out our hearts to the Lord, we knew that God heard our request. Obeying the scripture Dr. Ray would awaken us early in the morning to pray often quoting the scripture, *"I love them that love me; and those that seek me early shall find me. " Proverbs 8:17*

After developing her ministry of prayer, it wasn't long before my mother began teaching her children, all of the aspects and principles of prayer. For a season she passionately instilled teachings concerning the facets of prayer that remain with us today. We learned that Prayer is a unique opportunity to communicate with a Living God. Prayer is an expression of our sincere love and abiding trust in God. It is a joy to speak to Him and to quietly listen. *Ephesians 6:18* says, *to pray always with all prayer and supplication in the spirit, and watching thereunto with all perseverance and supplication for the saints.*

Perseverance creates a relentless pursuit to reach for God with compassion for others. It indicates a steady course of action, persistent in praying for the needs of others. Supplication on the other hand, is to entreat the Lord with a request or petition for help, on behalf of individuals who the Holy Spirit places upon your heart.

I've learned that intercession is an instance of actually praying to the Lord on behalf of another. It is also the act of communicating with God, humbly entreating Him for intervention, mediation or interposing His mercy for another. I genuinely believe that intercessors are very special because they are instruments of the Lord. I've often compared them to a bridge. A bridge is a structure spanning a particular distance providing passage. It is a connecting transition, an intermediate route or phase between two adjacent localities. Intercessors selflessly extend themselves to others, like a bridge, they are positioned to help, support and to provide stability in progressing from one place to another. *I exhort therefore, that, first of all, supplications, prayers, intercessions, and giving of thanks, be made for all men. I Timothy 2:1*

As we reflect on the teachings, I recall that there was great emphasis placed upon the need to have a pure heart; like David, *Create in me a clean heart, O God; and renew a right spirit within me. Psalms 51:10.* As Joseph, it was emphasized to have a true hearts of forgiveness. *So shall ye say unto Joseph, Forgive, I pray thee now, the trespass of thy brethren, and their sin; for they did unto thee evil: and now, we pray thee, forgive the trespass of the servants of the God of thy father. And Joseph wept when they spake unto him. Genesis 50:1*

We learned quite early that there are particular hindrances to answered prayers. Unresolved issues, offenses and unforgiveness in the heart are grievous to the Holy Spirit. These things must be confronted in order to have a reciprocal relationship with the Lord. *Confess your faults one to another, and pray one for another, that ye may be healed. The effectual fervent prayer of a righteous man availeth much. James 5:16*

Spiritual warfare is simply a description of conflict between unrelenting opposing forces. A reality of the Christian walk is the fact that; *we wrestle not against flesh and blood, but against principalities, against powers, against the rulers of the darkness of this world, against spiritual wickedness in high places. Ephesians 6:12.* The good news is that we have been equipped with spiritual weapons to overcome the strategies of the enemy. We are more than conquerors.

I believe that some of the greatest weapons against the enemy are, the power of the blood of Jesus, fasting and a consecrated prayer life. Warfare is the act of utilizing spiritual weapons. *Verily I say unto you, Whatsoever ye shall bind on earth shall be bound in heaven: and whatsoever ye shall loose on earth shall be loosed in heaven. Matthew 18:18*

We operate from a position of authority during spiritual warfare prayer. Note *Isaiah 54:17, No weapon that is formed against thee shall prosper; and every tongue that shall rise against thee in judgment thou shalt condemn. This is the heritage of the servants of the LORD, and their righteousness is of me, saith the LORD.*

Paul the Apostle charged a young Pastor Timothy that *thou mightest war a good warfare. I Timothy 1:18* and *call to remembrance the unfeigned faith that is in thee, which dwelt first in thy grandmother Lois, and thy mother Eunice, and I am persuaded that it's in thee also. II Timothy 1:5.* Unfeigned faith is a description of a sincere and genuine expression of one's faith.

To the church at Corinth Paul writes *(For the weapons of our warfare are not carnal, but mighty through God to the pulling down of strong holds;). Casting down imaginations, and every high thing that exalteth itself against the knowledge of God, and bringing into captivity every thought to the obedience of Christ;*

II Corinthians 10:4-5

At times we find ourselves confronted with serious prayer needs and I have been asked countless times by individuals searching to know, "How do I pray? What do I say? Where do I begin?"

As an Evangelist for over 20 years, I have found a common fiber in most requests for prayer. There have been countless thousands of request in the area of the family, including broken family relationships and blended family concerns. A great deal of requests has come in the area of financial crisis. There is also a common request for prayer in the area of emotional and physical healing. Recently there has been an increase requesting prayer for the Favor of God. Frequently we are asked for prayer concerning a spirit of consecration, fasting and a committed prayer life.

As you read the content of *"Prevailing Prayers of the Bible"*, embrace the faith of *Abraham*, as God reveals direction and instruction. Be inspired by the fiery plea of **Moses** for mercy. Despite ridicule, discover the amazing results of the persistent prayers of *Hannah*. Experience the awe-inspiring courage of *Esther*. Consider the words of *Jonah* as he prayed for deliverance. Be transformed by *Paul's* devotion. Examine the intensity of *Jesus* as he prayed in the Garden of Gethsemane. These are just a few examples of the actual individual prayers spoken in the Word of God. The Lord has given me this wonderful desire to share with the body of Christ the remarkable prayers of the Bible. This book is designed to share scriptural dialogue spoken from individuals recorded in the sacred pages of the Bible.

It is my greatest hope that you can reference these biblical prayers as guidelines to build your personal time with God. In addition, I pray that you will also glean from the prayers, a spirit of true worship and a heart of gratitude unto the Lord for answered prayers.

Identify with the words spoken in the *"Prevailing Prayers of the Bible"* and incorporate the extraordinary content into your personal prayer time.

The Wailing Wall

In the city of Jerusalem there remains an ancient remnant from the times of antiquity. This is the retaining wall that underlay the second temple in Jerusalem. The Western Wall is considered Holy and Sacred because it is the only remaining portion of the temple built by King Solomon. According to history, it is the remaining wall that was closest to the Holy of Holies. It is referred to as the Wailing Wall, because of Jews mourning the destruction of the temple. Presently the Wailing Wall is a gathering place and the site of pilgrimages, lamentations and praying people from around the world.

I remember having the privilege of standing at the Ancient Wailing Wall to pray. Men and women could be found praying at the wall every hour. There is a Mechitzas, or divider, that separates the men's section from the women. I will never forget the awesome presence of God. I can honestly say I sensed an indescribable awe as I witnessed people praying and pouring out their hearts to a living God.

As an eyewitness I was completely fascinated by one tradition I observed, where people placed slips of paper with prayer requests into the crevices of the wall. Looking closely I could see thousands of tiny folded papers embedded within every available space. This was an astonishing indication of their passion expressed to God through prayer.

I remember seeing individuals with prayer shawls, the tallit is traditionally worn during the time of morning service. The shawl is special to the Jewish people and is regarded with great respect. It represents a mantle of Holiness. The knotted fringes known as tzitzit are attached to its four corners. The purpose of the fringes serve as a reminder of the commandments of God. I pray that as you read ***"The Prevailing Prayers of the Bible",*** that you will glean from the magnificent prayers and be strengthened during your personal prayer time.

Contents

The Prayer of ...

Abraham.. 23

Joseph.. 27

Isaac 28

Rebekah 28

Jacob 29

Moses 32

Joshua 48

Gideon.. 51

Manoah... 52

Samson... 53

Hannah... 55

Samuel 57

David... 58

Solomon.. 61

Elijah.. 63

Elisha.. 65

Jehoahaz... 67

Hezekiah... 68

Jabez.. 70

Reubenites... 71

Judah.. 72

Jehoshaphat 73

Manasseh.. 75

Ezra.. 76

Nehemiah.. 78

Esther... 80

Job... 81

Prayer of the Psalms.............................. 82

Isaiah 87

Jeremiah... 88

Ezekiel.. 90

Daniel... 92

Jonah.. 94

Habakkuk.. 96

The Lord's Prayer............................ 99

Jesus.. 100

Zechariah.. 111

Stephen... 112

Peter... 112

Paul.. 115

Timothy... 125

Philemon... 126

Hebrews.. 127

James.. 128

Revelation.. 130

Abraham Father of a great multitude

"Lord, God What will thou give me seeing I go childless"

Genesis 15:1-18

¹ After these things the word of the LORD came unto Abram in a vision, saying, Fear not, Abram: I am thy shield, and thy exceeding great reward.

²And Abram said, LORD God, what wilt thou give me, seeing I go childless, and the steward of my house is this Eliezer of Damascus?

³And Abram said, Behold, to me thou hast given no seed: and, lo, one born in my house is mine heir.

⁴And, behold, the word of the LORD came unto him, saying, This shall not be thine heir; but he that shall come forth out of thine own bowels shall be thine heir.

⁵And he brought him forth abroad, and said, Look now toward heaven, and tell the stars, if thou be able to number them: and he said unto him, So shall thy seed be.

23

⁶And he believed in the LORD; and he counted it to him for righteousness.

⁷And he said unto him, I am the LORD that brought thee out of Ur of the Chaldees, to give thee this land to inherit it.

⁸And he said, LORD God, whereby shall I know that I shall inherit it?

⁹And he said unto him, Take me an heifer of three years old, and a she goat of three years old, and a ram of three years old, and a turtledove, and a young pigeon.

¹⁰And he took unto him all these, and divided them in the midst, and laid each piece one against another: but the birds divided he not.

¹¹And when the fowls came down upon the carcases, Abram drove them away.

¹²And when the sun was going down, a deep sleep fell upon Abram; and, lo, an horror of great darkness fell upon him.

¹³And he said unto Abram, Know of a surety that thy seed shall be a stranger in a land that is not theirs, and shall serve them; and they shall afflict them four hundred years;

¹⁴And also that nation, whom they shall serve, will I judge: and afterward shall they come out with great substance.

[15] And thou shalt go to thy fathers in peace; thou shalt be buried in a good old age.

[16] But in the fourth generation they shall come hither again: for the iniquity of the Amorites is not yet full.

[17] And it came to pass, that, when the sun went down, and it was dark, behold a smoking furnace, and a burning lamp that passed between those pieces.

[18] In the same day the LORD made a covenant with Abram, saying, Unto thy seed have I given this land, from the river of Egypt unto the great river, the river Euphrates:

"Wilt thou destroy the righteous with the Wicked"

Genesis 18:20-33

[20] And the LORD said, Because the cry of Sodom and Gomorrah is great, and because their sin is very grievous;

[21] I will go down now, and see whether they have done altogether according to the cry of it, which is come unto me; and if not, I will know.

[22] And the men turned their faces from thence, and went toward Sodom: but Abraham stood yet before the LORD.

[23] And Abraham drew near, and said, Wilt thou also destroy the righteous with the wicked?

[17]*So Abraham prayed unto God: and God healed Abimelech, and his wife, and his maidservants; and they bare children.*

"Abraham's servant prays for Success"

Genesis 24:17-19

[17]*And the servant ran to meet her, and said, Let me, I pray thee, drink a little water of thy pitcher.*

[18]*And she said, Drink, my lord: and she hasted, and let down her pitcher upon her hand, and gave him drink.*

[19]*And when she had done giving him drink, she said, I will draw water for thy camels also, until they have done drinking.*

Joseph *increase; addition*

"Joseph's Prayer of Forgiveness"

Genesis 50:17-20

¹⁷So shall ye say unto Joseph, Forgive, I pray thee now, the trespass of thy brethren, and their sin; for they did unto thee evil: and now, we pray thee, forgive the trespass of the servants of the God of thy father. And Joseph wept when they spake unto him.

¹⁸And his brethren also went and fell down before his face; and they said, Behold, we be thy servants.

¹⁹And Joseph said unto them, Fear not: for am I in the place of God?

²⁰But as for you, ye thought evil against me; but God meant it unto good, to bring to pass, as it is this day to save much people alive.

Isaac laughter

"Isaac intreated the Lord for his wife"

Genesis 25:21

²¹ *And Isaac intreated the LORD for his wife, because she was barren: and the LORD was intreated of him, and Rebekah his wife conceived.*

Rebekah fat; fattened; a quarrel appeased

"If it be so, why am I thus"

Genesis 25:22-26

²² *And the children struggled together within her; and she said, If it be so, why am I thus? And she went to enquire of the LORD.*

[23]And the LORD said unto her, Two nations are in thy womb, and two manner of people shall be separated from thy bowels; and the one people shall be stronger than the other people; and the elder shall serve the younger.

[24]And when her days to be delivered were fulfilled, behold, there were twins in her womb.

[25]And the first came out red, all over like an hairy garment; and they called his name Esau.

[26]And after that came his brother out, and his hand took hold on Esau's heel; and his name was called Jacob: and Isaac was threescore years old when she bare them.

Jacob **that displaces, substitute for another, the heel**

"Jacob prays for deliverance from Esau"

Genesis 32:9-12

[9]And Jacob said, O God of my father Abraham, and God of my father Isaac, the LORD which saidst unto me, Return unto thy country, and to thy kindred, and I will deal well with thee:

29

[10]I am not worthy of the least of all the mercies, and of all the truth, which thou hast shewed unto thy servant; for with my staff I passed over this Jordan; and now I am become two bands.

[11]Deliver me, I pray thee, from the hand of my brother, from the hand of Esau: for I fear him, lest he will come and smite me, and the mother with the children.

[12]And thou saidst, I will surely do thee good, and make thy seed as the sand of the sea, which cannot be numbered for multitude.

"Jacob for I have seen God face to face"

Genesis 32:22-31

[22]And he rose up that night, and took his two wives, and his two womenservants, and his eleven sons, and passed over the ford Jabbok.

[23]And he took them, and sent them over the brook, and sent over that he had.

[24]And Jacob was left alone; and there wrestled a man with him until the breaking of the day.

[25]And when he saw that he prevailed not against him, he touched the hollow of his thigh; and the hollow of Jacob's thigh was out of joint, as he wrestled with him.

[26]And he said, Let me go, for the day breaketh. And he said, I will not let thee go, except thou bless me.

²⁷And he said unto him, What is thy name? And he said, Jacob.

²⁸And he said, Thy name shall be called no more Jacob, but Israel: for as a prince hast thou power with God and with men, and hast prevailed.

²⁹And Jacob asked him, and said, Tell me, I pray thee, thy name. And he said, Wherefore is it that thou dost ask after my name? And he blessed him there.

³⁰And Jacob called the name of the place Peniel: for I have seen God face to face, and my life is preserved.

³¹And as he passed over Penuel the sun rose upon him, and he halted upon his thigh.

"And the children of Israel sighed by reason of the bondage"

Exodus 2:23-25

²³And it came to pass in process of time, that the king of Egypt died: and the children of Israel sighed by reason of the bondage, and they cried, and their cry came up unto God by reason of the bondage.

²⁴And God heard their groaning, and God remembered his covenant with Abraham, with Isaac, and with Jacob.

²⁵And God looked upon the children of Israel, and God had respect unto them.

31

Moses *taken out; drawn forth*

"Who Am I that I should go"

Exodus 3:1-21

¹*N*ow Moses kept the flock of Jethro his father in law, the priest of Midian: and he led the flock to the backside of the desert, and came to the mountain of God, even to Horeb.

²And the angel of the LORD appeared unto him in a flame of fire out of the midst of a bush: and he looked, and, behold, the bush burned with fire, and the bush was not consumed.

³And Moses said, I will now turn aside, and see this great sight, why the bush is not burnt.

⁴And when the LORD saw that he turned aside to see, God called unto him out of the midst of the bush, and said, Moses, Moses. And he said, Here am I.

⁵And he said, Draw not nigh hither: put off thy shoes from off thy feet, for the place whereon thou standest is holy ground.

[6]Moreover he said, I am the God of thy father, the God of Abraham, the God of Isaac, and the God of Jacob. And Moses hid his face; for he was afraid to look upon God.

[7]And the LORD said, I have surely seen the affliction of my people which are in Egypt, and have heard their cry by reason of their taskmasters; for I know their sorrows;

[8]And I am come down to deliver them out of the hand of the Egyptians, and to bring them up out of that land unto a good land and a large, unto a land flowing with milk and honey; unto the place of the Canaanites, and the Hittites, and the Amorites, and the Perizzites, and the Hivites, and the Jebusites.

[9]Now therefore, behold, the cry of the children of Israel is come unto me: and I have also seen the oppression wherewith the Egyptians oppress them.

[10]Come now therefore, and I will send thee unto Pharaoh, that thou mayest bring forth my people the children of Israel out of Egypt.

[11]And Moses said unto God, Who am I, that I should go unto Pharaoh, and that I should bring forth the children of Israel out of Egypt?

[12]And he said, Certainly I will be with thee; and this shall be a token unto thee, that I have sent thee: When

thou hast brought forth the people out of Egypt, ye shall serve God upon this mountain.

¹³And Moses said unto God, Behold, when I come unto the children of Israel, and shall say unto them, The God of your fathers hath sent me unto you; and they shall say to me, What is his name? what shall I say unto them?

¹⁴And God said unto Moses, I AM THAT I AM: and he said, Thus shalt thou say unto the children of Israel, I AM hath sent me unto you.

¹⁵And God said moreover unto Moses, Thus shalt thou say unto the children of Israel, the LORD God of your fathers, the God of Abraham, the God of Isaac, and the God of Jacob, hath sent me unto you: this is my name for ever, and this is my memorial unto all generations.

¹⁶Go, and gather the elders of Israel together, and say unto them, The LORD God of your fathers, the God of Abraham, of Isaac, and of Jacob, appeared unto me, saying, I have surely visited you, and seen that which is done to you in Egypt:

¹⁷And I have said, I will bring you up out of the affliction of Egypt unto the land of the Canaanites, and the Hittites, and the Amorites, and the Perizzites, and the Hivites, and the Jebusites, unto a land flowing with milk and honey.

¹⁸And they shall hearken to thy voice: and thou shalt come, thou and the elders of Israel, unto the king of

Egypt, and ye shall say unto him, The LORD God of the Hebrews hath met with us: and now let us go, we beseech thee, three days' journey into the wilderness, that we may sacrifice to the LORD our God.

[19] And I am sure that the king of Egypt will not let you go, no, not by a mighty hand.

[20] And I will stretch out my hand, and smite Egypt with all my wonders which I will do in the midst thereof: and after that he will let you go.

[21] And I will give this people favour in the sight of the Egyptians: and it shall come to pass, that, when ye go, ye shall not go empty.

"Behold they will not believe me"

Exodus 4:1-17

[1] And Moses answered and said, But, behold, they will not believe me, nor hearken unto my voice: for they will say, The LORD hath not appeared unto thee.

[2] And the LORD said unto him, What is that in thine hand? And he said, A rod.

[3] And he said, Cast it on the ground. And he cast it on the ground, and it became a serpent; and Moses fled from before it.

⁴And the LORD said unto Moses, Put forth thine hand, and take it by the tail. And he put forth his hand, and caught it, and it became a rod in his hand:

⁵That they may believe that the LORD God of their fathers, the God of Abraham, the God of Isaac, and the God of Jacob, hath appeared unto thee.

⁶And the LORD said furthermore unto him, Put now thine hand into thy bosom. And he put his hand into his bosom: and when he took it out, behold, his hand was leprous as snow.

⁷And he said, Put thine hand into thy bosom again. And he put his hand into his bosom again; and plucked it out of his bosom, and, behold, it was turned again as his other flesh.

⁸And it shall come to pass, if they will not believe thee, neither hearken to the voice of the first sign, that they will believe the voice of the latter sign.

⁹And it shall come to pass, if they will not believe also these two signs, neither hearken unto thy voice, that thou shalt take of the water of the river, and pour it upon the dry land: and the water which thou takest out of the river shall become blood upon the dry land.

¹⁰And Moses said unto the LORD, O my LORD, I am not eloquent, neither heretofore, nor since thou hast spoken unto thy servant: but I am slow of speech, and of a slow tongue.

[11]*And the LORD said unto him, Who hath made man's mouth? or who maketh the dumb, or deaf, or the seeing, or the blind? have not I the LORD?*

[12]*Now therefore go, and I will be with thy mouth, and teach thee what thou shalt say.*

[13]*And he said, O my LORD, send, I pray thee, by the hand of him whom thou wilt send.*

[14]*And the anger of the LORD was kindled against Moses, and he said, Is not Aaron the Levite thy brother? I know that he can speak well. And also, behold, he cometh forth to meet thee: and when he seeth thee, he will be glad in his heart.*

[15]*And thou shalt speak unto him, and put words in his mouth: and I will be with thy mouth, and with his mouth, and will teach you what ye shall do.*

[16]*And he shall be thy spokesman unto the people: and he shall be, even he shall be to thee instead of a mouth, and thou shalt be to him instead of God.*

[17]*And thou shalt take this rod in thine hand, wherewith thou shalt do signs.*

Exodus 8:9-15

⁹*And Moses said unto Pharaoh, Glory over me: when shall I intreat for thee, and for thy servants, and for thy people, to destroy the frogs from thee and thy houses, that they may remain in the river only?*

¹⁰*And he said, To morrow. And he said, Be it according to thy word: that thou mayest know that there is none like unto the LORD our God.*

¹¹*And the frogs shall depart from thee, and from thy houses, and from thy servants, and from thy people; they shall remain in the river only.*

¹²*And Moses and Aaron went out from Pharaoh: and Moses cried unto the LORD because of the frogs which he had brought against Pharaoh.*

¹³*And the LORD did according to the word of Moses; and the frogs died out of the houses, out of the villages, and out of the fields.*

¹⁴*And they gathered them together upon heaps: and the land stank.*

¹⁵*But when Pharaoh saw that there was respite, he hardened his heart, and hearkened not unto them; as the LORD had said.*

"And he cried unto the Lord and the Lord shewed him"

Exodus 15:22-25

22 So Moses brought Israel from the Red sea, and they went out into the wilderness of Shur; and they went three days in the wilderness, and found no water.

23 And when they came to Marah, they could not drink of the waters of Marah, for they were bitter: therefore the name of it was called Marah.

24 And the people murmured against Moses, saying, What shall we drink?

25 And he cried unto the LORD; and the LORD shewed him a tree, which when he had cast into the waters, the waters were made sweet: there he made for them a statute and an ordinance, and there he proved them,

"What shall I do unto this people"

Exodus 17:3-7

3 And the people thirsted there for water; and the people murmured against Moses, and said, Wherefore is this that thou hast brought us up out of Egypt, to kill us and our children and our cattle with thirst?

4 And Moses cried unto the LORD, saying, What shall I do unto this people? they be almost ready to stone me.

5 And the LORD said unto Moses, Go on before the people, and take with thee of the elders of Israel; and

39

thy rod, wherewith thou smotest the river, take in thine hand, and go.

⁶Behold, I will stand before thee there upon the rock in Horeb; and thou shalt smite the rock, and there shall come water out of it, that the people may drink. And Moses did so in the sight of the elders of Israel.

⁷And he called the name of the place Massah, and Meribah, because of the chiding of the children of Israel, and because they tempted the LORD, saying, Is the LORD among us, or not?

"Oh, this people have sinned a great sin"

Exodus 32:30-35

³⁰And it came to pass on the morrow, that Moses said unto the people, Ye have sinned a great sin: and now I will go up unto the LORD; peradventure I shall make an atonement for your sin.

³¹And Moses returned unto the LORD, and said, Oh, this people have sinned a great sin, and have made them gods of gold.

³²Yet now, if thou wilt forgive their sin--; and if not, blot me, I pray thee, out of thy book which thou hast written.

³³And the LORD said unto Moses, Whosoever hath sinned against me, him will I blot out of my book.

^{34}*Therefore now go, lead the people unto the place of which I have spoken unto thee: behold, mine Angel shall go before thee: nevertheless in the day when I visit I will visit their sin upon them.*

^{35}*And the LORD plagued the people, because they made the calf, which Aaron made.*

"The Lord make His face shine upon thee"

Numbers 6:24-26

^{24}*The Lord bless thee, and keep thee:*

^{25}*The Lord make his face shine upon thee, and be gracious unto thee*

^{26}*The Lord lift up his countenance upon thee and give thee peace.*

"Kill me; I pray thee"

Numbers 11:10-23

^{10}*Then Moses heard the people weep throughout their families, every man in the door of his tent: and the anger of the LORD was kindled greatly; Moses also was displeased.*

^{11}*And Moses said unto the LORD, Wherefore hast thou afflicted thy servant? and wherefore have I not found favour in thy sight, that thou layest the burden of all this people upon me?*

¹²Have I conceived all this people? have I begotten them, that thou shouldest say unto me, Carry them in thy bosom, as a nursing father beareth the sucking child, unto the land which thou swarest unto their fathers?

¹³Whence should I have flesh to give unto all this people? for they weep unto me, saying, Give us flesh, that we may eat.

¹⁴I am not able to bear all this people alone, because it is too heavy for me.

¹⁵And if thou deal thus with me, kill me, I pray thee, out of hand, if I have found favour in thy sight; and let me not see my wretchedness.

¹⁶And the LORD said unto Moses, Gather unto me seventy men of the elders of Israel, whom thou knowest to be the elders of the people, and officers over them; and bring them unto the tabernacle of the congregation, that they may stand there with thee.

¹⁷And I will come down and talk with thee there: and I will take of the spirit which is upon thee, and will put it upon them; and they shall bear the burden of the people with thee, that thou bear it not thyself alone.

¹⁸And say thou unto the people, Sanctify yourselves against to morrow, and ye shall eat flesh: for ye have wept in the ears of the LORD, saying, Who shall give us flesh to eat? for it was well with us in Egypt: therefore the LORD will give you flesh, and ye shall eat.

[19]Ye shall not eat one day, nor two days, nor five days, neither ten days, nor twenty days;

[20]But even a whole month, until it come out at your nostrils, and it be loathsome unto you: because that ye have despised the LORD which is among you, and have wept before him, saying, Why came we forth out of Egypt?

[21]And Moses said, The people, among whom I am, are six hundred thousand footmen; and thou hast said, I will give them flesh, that they may eat a whole month.

[22]Shall the flocks and the herds be slain for them, to suffice them? or shall all the fish of the sea be gathered together for them, to suffice them?

[23]And the LORD said unto Moses, Is the LORD'S hand waxed short? thou shalt see now whether my word shall come to pass unto thee or not.

"Moses Prayer for Miriam, Heal her now"

Numbers 12:1-14

[1]And Miriam and Aaron spake against Moses because of the Ethiopian woman whom he had married: for he had married an Ethiopian woman.

[2]And they said, Hath the LORD indeed spoken only by Moses? hath he not spoken also by us? And the LORD heard it.

³(Now the man Moses was very meek, above all the men which were upon the face of the earth.)

⁴And the LORD spake suddenly unto Moses, and unto Aaron, and unto Miriam, Come out ye three unto the tabernacle of the congregation. And they three came out.

⁵And the LORD came down in the pillar of the cloud, and stood in the door of the tabernacle, and called Aaron and Miriam: and they both came forth.

⁶And he said, Hear now my words: If there be a prophet among you, I the LORD will make myself known unto him in a vision, and will speak unto him in a dream.

⁷My servant Moses is not so, who is faithful in all mine house.

⁸With him will I speak mouth to mouth, even apparently, and not in dark speeches; and the similitude of the LORD shall he behold: wherefore then were ye not afraid to speak against my servant Moses?

⁹And the anger of the LORD was kindled against them; and he departed.

¹⁰And the cloud departed from off the tabernacle; and, behold, Miriam became leprous, white as snow: and Aaron looked upon Miriam, and, behold, she was leprous.

[11]And Aaron said unto Moses, Alas, my lord, I beseech thee, lay not the sin upon us, wherein we have done foolishly, and wherein we have sinned.

[12]Let her not be as one dead, of whom the flesh is half consumed when he cometh out of his mother's womb.

[13]And Moses cried unto the LORD, saying, Heal her now, O God, I beseech thee.

[14]And the LORD said unto Moses, If her father had but spit in her face, should she not be ashamed seven days? let her be shut out from the camp seven days, and after that let her be received in again.

"Let the Lord set a man over the Congregation"

Numbers 27:15-22

[15]And Moses spake unto the LORD, saying,

[16]Let the LORD, the God of the spirits of all flesh, set a man over the congregation,

[17]Which may go out before them, and which may go in before them, and which may lead them out, and which may bring them in; that the congregation of the LORD be not as sheep which have no shepherd.

[18]And the LORD said unto Moses, Take thee Joshua the son of Nun, a man in whom is the spirit, and lay thine hand upon him;

¹⁹*And set him before Eleazar the priest, and before all the congregation; and give him a charge in their sight.*

²⁰*And thou shalt put some of thine honour upon him, that all the congregation of the children of Israel may be obedient.*

²¹*And he shall stand before Eleazar the priest, who shall ask counsel for him after the judgment of Urim before the LORD: at his word shall they go out, and at his word they shall come in, both he, and all the children of Israel with him, even all the congregation.*

²²*And Moses did as the LORD commanded him: and he took Joshua, and set him before Eleazar the priest, and before all the congregation:*

"Moses prays that he may see the Promised Land"

Deuteronomy 3:23-24

²³*And I besought the LORD at that time, saying,*

²⁴*O Lord GOD, thou hast begun to shew thy servant thy greatness, and thy mighty hand: for what God is there in heaven or in earth, that can do according to thy works, and according to thy might?*

Deuteronomy 34:1-4

¹*And Moses went up from the plains of Moab unto the mountain of Nebo, to the top of Pisgah, that is over*

against Jericho. And the LORD shewed him all the land of Gilead, unto Dan,

²And all Naphtali, and the land of Ephraim, and Manasseh, and all the land of Judah, unto the utmost sea,

³And the south, and the plain of the valley of Jericho, the city of palm trees, unto Zoar.

⁴And the LORD said unto him, This is the land which I sware unto Abraham, unto Isaac, and unto Jacob, saying, I will give it unto thy seed: I have caused thee to see it with thine eyes, but thou shalt not go over thither.

The Shema *hearing, obeying*

"A Jewish Prayer"

Deuteronomy 6:4-9

⁴*H*ear, O Israel: The LORD our God is one LORD:

⁵And thou shalt love the LORD thy God with all thine heart, and with all thy soul, and with all thy might.

⁶And these words, which I command thee this day, shall be in thine heart:

⁷And thou shalt teach them diligently unto thy children, and shalt talk of them when thou sittest in thine house, and when thou walkest by the way, and when thou liest down, and when thou risest up.

⁸And thou shalt bind them for a sign upon thine hand, and they shall be as frontlets between thine eyes.

⁹And thou shalt write them upon the posts of thy house, and on thy gates.

Joshua a savior; a deliverer

"Joshua prays for help"

Joshua 7:6-13

⁶And Joshua rent his clothes, and fell to the earth upon his face before the ark of the LORD until the eventide, he and the elders of Israel, and put dust upon their heads.

⁷And Joshua said, Alas, O LORD God, wherefore hast thou at all brought this people over Jordan, to deliver us

48

into the hand of the Amorites, to destroy us? would to God we had been content, and dwelt on the other side Jordan!

[8]O LORD, what shall I say, when Israel turneth their backs before their enemies!

[9]For the Canaanites and all the inhabitants of the land shall hear of it, and shall environ us round, and cut off our name from the earth: and what wilt thou do unto thy great name?

[10]And the LORD said unto Joshua, Get thee up; wherefore liest thou thus upon thy face?

[11]Israel hath sinned, and they have also transgressed my covenant which I commanded them: for they have even taken of the accursed thing, and have also stolen, and dissembled also, and they have put it even among their own stuff.

[12]Therefore the children of Israel could not stand before their enemies, but turned their backs before their enemies, because they were accursed: neither will I be with you any more, except ye destroy the accursed from among you.

[13]Up, sanctify the people, and say, Sanctify yourselves against to morrow: for thus saith the LORD God of Israel, There is an accursed thing in the midst of thee, O Israel: thou canst not stand before thine enemies, until ye take away the accursed thing from among you.

¹²*Then spake Joshua to the LORD in the day when the LORD delivered up the Amorites before the children of Israel, and he said in the sight of Israel, Sun, stand thou still upon Gibeon; and thou, Moon, in the valley of Ajalon.*

¹³*And the sun stood still, and the moon stayed, until the people had avenged themselves upon their enemies. Is not this written in the book of Jasher? So the sun stood still in the midst of heaven, and hasted not to go down about a whole day.*

¹⁴*And there was no day like that before it or after it, that the LORD hearkened unto the voice of a man: for the LORD fought for Israel.*

Gideon *he that bruises or breaks; a destroyer*

"Let me prove I pray thee this once with fleece"

Judges 6:36-40

³⁶ And Gideon said unto God, If thou wilt save Israel by mine hand, as thou hast said,

³⁷ Behold, I will put a fleece of wool in the floor; and if the dew be on the fleece only, and it be dry upon all the earth beside, then shall I know that thou wilt save Israel by mine hand, as thou hast said.

³⁸ And it was so: for he rose up early on the morrow, and thrust the fleece together, and wringed the dew out of the fleece, a bowl full of water.

³⁹ And Gideon said unto God, Let not thine anger be hot against me, and I will speak but this once: let me prove, I pray thee, but this once with the fleece; let it now be dry only upon the fleece, and upon all the ground let there be dew.

⁴⁰ And God did so that night: for it was dry upon the fleece only, and there was dew on all the ground.

51

 *rest; a present*

"Manoah, the father of Samson, prays for Divine Guidance"

Judges 13:8-14

⁸*Then Manoah intreated the LORD, and said, O my Lord, let the man of God which thou didst send come again unto us, and teach us what we shall do unto the child that shall be born.*

⁹*And God hearkened to the voice of Manoah; and the angel of God came again unto the woman as she sat in the field: but Manoah her husband was not with her.*

¹⁰*And the woman made haste, and ran, and shewed her husband, and said unto him, Behold, the man hath appeared unto me, that came unto me the other day.*

¹¹*And Manoah arose, and went after his wife, and came to the man, and said unto him, Art thou the man that spakest unto the woman? And he said, I am.*

¹²*And Manoah said, Now let thy words come to pass. How shall we order the child, and how shall we do unto him?*

[13] And the angel of the LORD said unto Manoah, Of all that I said unto the woman let her beware.

[14] She may not eat of any thing that cometh of the vine, neither let her drink wine or strong drink, nor eat any unclean thing: all that I commanded her let her observe.

Samson **his sun; his service; there the second time**

"And Samson thirst and called on the Lord"

Judges 15:18-19

[18] And he was sore athirst, and called on the LORD, and said, Thou hast given this great deliverance into the hand of thy servant: and now shall I die for thirst, and fall into the hand of the uncircumcised?

[19] But God clave an hollow place that was in the jaw, and there came water thereout; and when he had drunk, his spirit came again, and he revived: wherefore he called the name thereof Enhakkore, which is in Lehi unto this day.

[28]And Samson called unto the LORD, and said, O Lord God, remember me, I pray thee, and strengthen me, I pray thee, only this once, O God, that I may be at once avenged of the Philistines for my two eyes.

[29]And Samson took hold of the two middle pillars upon which the house stood, and on which it was borne up, of the one with his right hand, and of the other with his left.

[30]And Samson said, Let me die with the Philistines. And he bowed himself with all his might; and the house fell upon the lords, and upon all the people that were therein. So the dead which he slew at his death were more than they which he slew in his life.

Hannah **gracious; merciful; she that gives**

"In bitterness of soul Hannah wept for a son"

I Samuel 1:10-17 & 20

[10] *And she was in bitterness of soul, and prayed unto the LORD, and wept sore.*

[11] *And she vowed a vow, and said, O LORD of hosts, if thou wilt indeed look on the affliction of thine handmaid, and remember me, and not forget thine handmaid, but wilt give unto thine handmaid a man child, then I will give him unto the LORD all the days of his life, and there shall no razor come upon his head.*

[12] *And it came to pass, as she continued praying before the LORD, that Eli marked her mouth.*

[13] *Now Hannah, she spake in her heart; only her lips moved, but her voice was not heard: therefore Eli thought she had been drunken.*

[14] *And Eli said unto her, How long wilt thou be drunken? put away thy wine from thee.*

[15]And Hannah answered and said, No, my lord, I am a woman of a sorrowful spirit: I have drunk neither wine nor strong drink, but have poured out my soul before the LORD.

[16]Count not thine handmaid for a daughter of Belial: for out of the abundance of my complaint and grief have I spoken hitherto.

[17]Then Eli answered and said, Go in peace: and the God of Israel grant thee thy petition that thou hast asked of him.

[20]Wherefore it came to pass, when the time was come about after Hannah had conceived, that she bare a son, and called his name Samuel, saying, Because I have asked him of the LORD.

"My heart rejoiceth in the Lord"

2 Samuel 2:1

[1]And Hannah prayed, and said, My heart rejoiceth in the LORD, mine horn is exalted in the LORD: my mouth is enlarged over mine enemies; because I rejoice in thy salvation.

Samuel *lent of God; heard of God; asked of God*

"And Samuel Cried unto the Lord for Israel"

I Samuel 7:5-12

⁵ *And Samuel said, Gather all Israel to Mizpeh, and I will pray for you unto the LORD.*

⁶*And they gathered together to Mizpeh, and drew water, and poured it out before the LORD, and fasted on that day, and said there, We have sinned against the LORD. And Samuel judged the children of Israel in Mizpeh.*

⁷*And when the Philistines heard that the children of Israel were gathered together to Mizpeh, the lords of the Philistines went up against Israel. And when the children of Israel heard it, they were afraid of the Philistines.*

⁸*And the children of Israel said to Samuel, Cease not to cry unto the LORD our God for us, that he will save us out of the hand of the Philistines.*

[9] And Samuel took a sucking lamb, and offered it for a burnt offering wholly unto the LORD: and Samuel cried unto the LORD for Israel; and the LORD heard him.

[10] And as Samuel was offering up the burnt offering, the Philistines drew near to battle against Israel: but the LORD thundered with a great thunder on that day upon the Philistines, and discomfited them; and they were smitten before Israel.

[11] And the men of Israel went out of Mizpeh, and pursued the Philistines, and smote them, until they came under Bethcar.

[12] Then Samuel took a stone, and set it between Mizpeh and Shen, and called the name of it Ebenezer, saying, Hitherto hath the LORD helped us.

David **well-beloved, dear**

"David inquired of the Lord for Guidance"

2 Samuel 7:18-29

[18] Then went king David in, and sat before the LORD, and he said, Who am I, O Lord GOD? and what is my house, that thou hast brought me hitherto?

58

[19]And this was yet a small thing in thy sight, O Lord GOD; but thou hast spoken also of thy servant's house for a great while to come. And is this the manner of man, O Lord GOD?

[20]And what can David say more unto thee? for thou, Lord GOD, knowest thy servant.

[21]For thy word's sake, and according to thine own heart, hast thou done all these great things, to make thy servant know them.

[22]Wherefore thou art great, O LORD God: for there is none like thee, neither is there any God beside thee, according to all that we have heard with our ears.

[23]And what one nation in the earth is like thy people, even like Israel, whom God went to redeem for a people to himself, and to make him a name, and to do for you great things and terrible, for thy land, before thy people, which thou redeemedst to thee from Egypt, from the nations and their gods?

[24]For thou hast confirmed to thyself thy people Israel to be a people unto thee for ever: and thou, LORD, art become their God.

[25]And now, O LORD God, the word that thou hast spoken concerning thy servant, and concerning his house, establish it for ever, and do as thou hast said.

*26*And let thy name be magnified for ever, saying, The LORD of hosts is the God over Israel: and let the house of thy servant David be established before thee.

*27*For thou, O LORD of hosts, God of Israel, hast revealed to thy servant, saying, I will build thee an house: therefore hath thy servant found in his heart to pray this prayer unto thee.

*28*And now, O Lord GOD, thou art that God, and thy words be true, and thou hast promised this goodness unto thy servant:

*29*Therefore now let it please thee to bless the house of thy servant, that it may continue for ever before thee: for thou, O Lord GOD, hast spoken it: and with thy blessing let the house of thy servant be blessed for ever.

"Oh, that I may have a drink of water"

I Chronicles 11:15-18

*15*Now three of the thirty captains went down to the rock to David, into the cave of Adullam; and the host of the Philistines encamped in the valley of Rephaim.

*16*And David was then in the hold, and the Philistines' garrison was then at Bethlehem.

*17*And David longed, and said, Oh that one would give me drink of the water of the well of Bethlehem, that is at the gate!

[18]*And the three brake through the host of the Philistines, and drew water out of the well of Bethlehem, that was by the gate, and took it, and brought it to David: but David would not drink of it, but poured it out to the LORD.*

Solomon, peaceable; perfect; one who recompenses

"Give thy Servant a wise and understanding heart"

I Kings 3:6-15

[6]*And Solomon said, Thou hast shewed unto thy servant David my father great mercy, according as he walked before thee in truth, and in righteousness, and in uprightness of heart with thee; and thou hast kept for him this great kindness, that thou hast given him a son to sit on his throne, as it is this day.*

[7]*And now, O LORD my God, thou hast made thy servant king instead of David my father: and I am but a little child: I know not how to go out or come in.*

[8]*And thy servant is in the midst of thy people which thou hast chosen, a great people, that cannot be numbered nor counted for multitude.*

^{9}Give therefore thy servant an understanding heart to judge thy people, that I may discern between good and bad: for who is able to judge this thy so great a people?

^{10}And the speech pleased the LORD, that Solomon had asked this thing.

^{11}And God said unto him, Because thou hast asked this thing, and hast not asked for thyself long life; neither hast asked riches for thyself, nor hast asked the life of thine enemies; but hast asked for thyself understanding to discern judgment;

^{12}Behold, I have done according to thy words: lo, I have given thee a wise and an understanding heart; so that there was none like thee before thee, neither after thee shall any arise like unto thee.

^{13}And I have also given thee that which thou hast not asked, both riches, and honour: so that there shall not be any among the kings like unto thee all thy days.

^{14}And if thou wilt walk in my ways, to keep my statutes and my commandments, as thy father David did walk, then I will lengthen thy days.

^{15}And Solomon awoke; and, behold, it was a dream. And he came to Jerusalem, and stood before the ark of the covenant of the LORD, and offered up burnt offerings, and offered peace offerings, and made a feast to all his servants.

Elijah **God the Lord, the strong Lord**

"O Lord God I pray thee, Let this child's soul come into him"

I Kings 17:20-23

[20] And he cried unto the LORD, and said, O LORD my God, hast thou also brought evil upon the widow with whom I sojourn, by slaying her son?

[21] And he stretched himself upon the child three times, and cried unto the LORD, and said, O LORD my God, I pray thee, let this child's soul come into him again.

[22] And the LORD heard the voice of Elijah; and the soul of the child came into him again, and he revived.

[23] And Elijah took the child, and brought him down out of the chamber into the house, and delivered him unto his mother: and Elijah said, See, thy son liveth.

"Elijah prays, Hear me O Lord, that this people may know that thou art God"

[36]*And it came to pass at the time of the offering of the evening sacrifice, that Elijah the prophet came near, and said, LORD God of Abraham, Isaac, and of Israel, let it be known this day that thou art God in Israel, and that I am thy servant, and that I have done all these things at thy word.*

[37]*Hear me, O LORD, hear me, that this people may know that thou art the LORD God, and that thou hast turned their heart back again.*

[38]*Then the fire of the LORD fell, and consumed the burnt sacrifice, and the wood, and the stones, and the dust, and licked up the water that was in the trench.*

[39]*And when all the people saw it, they fell on their faces: and they said, The LORD, he is the God; the LORD, he is the God.*

[40]*And Elijah said unto them, Take the prophets of Baal; let not one of them escape. And they took them: and Elijah brought them down to the brook Kishon, and slew them there.*

"Enough, Elijah prays for death under the Juniper Tree"

I Kings 19:4

⁴But he himself went a day's journey into the wilderness, and came and sat down under a juniper tree: and he requested for himself that he might die; and said, It is enough; now, O LORD, take away my life; for I am not better than my fathers.

Elisha Salvation of God

"Elisha prays, I pray thee open their eyes"

2 Kings 6:17-23

¹⁷And Elisha prayed, and said, LORD, I pray thee, open his eyes, that he may see. And the LORD opened the eyes of the young man; and he saw: and, behold, the mountain was full of horses and chariots of fire round about Elisha.

¹⁸And when they came down to him, Elisha prayed unto the LORD, and said, Smite this people, I pray thee, with blindness. And he smote them with blindness according to the word of Elisha.

¹⁹And Elisha said unto them, This is not the way, neither is this the city: follow me, and I will bring you to the man whom ye seek. But he led them to Samaria.

²⁰And it came to pass, when they were come into Samaria, that Elisha said, LORD, open the eyes of these men, that they may see. And the LORD opened their eyes, and they saw; and, behold, they were in the midst of Samaria.

²¹And the king of Israel said unto Elisha, when he saw them, My father, shall I smite them? shall I smite them?

²²And he answered, Thou shalt not smite them: wouldest thou smite those whom thou hast taken captive with thy sword and with thy bow? set bread and water before them, that they may eat and drink, and go to their master.

²³And he prepared great provision for them: and when they had eaten and drunk, he sent them away, and they went to their master. So the bands of Syria came no more into the land of Israel.

 **possession of Jehovah**

"Jehohahaz besought the Lord for freedom of oppression"

2 Kings 13:4-5

⁴*And Jehoahaz besought the LORD, and the LORD hearkened unto him: for he saw the oppression of Israel, because the king of Syria oppressed them.*

⁵*And the LORD gave Israel a saviour, so that they went out from under the hand of the Syrians: and the children of Israel dwelt in their tents, as beforetime.*

67

 **strength of the Lord**

"Hezekiah prayed that the kingdom of the earth will know that thou art God"

2 Kings 19:15-19

¹⁵*And Hezekiah prayed before the LORD, and said, O LORD God of Israel, which dwellest between the cherubims, thou art the God, even thou alone, of all the kingdoms of the earth; thou hast made heaven and earth.*

¹⁶*LORD, bow down thine ear, and hear: open, LORD, thine eyes, and see: and hear the words of Sennacherib, which hath sent him to reproach the living God.*

¹⁷*Of a truth, LORD, the kings of Assyria have destroyed the nations and their lands,*

¹⁸*And have cast their gods into the fire: for they were no gods, but the work of men's hands, wood and stone: therefore they have destroyed them.*

¹⁹*Now therefore, O LORD our God, I beseech thee, save thou us out of his hand, that all the kingdoms of the*

earth may know that thou art the LORD God, even thou only.

"Hezekiah turned his face to the wall and prayed for Deliverance"

2 Kings 20:1-6

[1]*In those days was Hezekiah sick unto death. And the prophet Isaiah the son of Amoz came to him, and said unto him, Thus saith the LORD, Set thine house in order; for thou shalt die, and not live.*

[2]*Then he turned his face to the wall, and prayed unto the LORD, saying,*

[3]*I beseech thee, O LORD, remember now how I have walked before thee in truth and with a perfect heart, and have done that which is good in thy sight. And Hezekiah wept sore.*

[4]*And it came to pass, afore Isaiah was gone out into the middle court, that the word of the LORD came to him, saying,*

[5]*Turn again, and tell Hezekiah the captain of my people, Thus saith the LORD, the God of David thy father, I have heard thy prayer, I have seen thy tears: behold, I will heal thee: on the third day thou shalt go up unto the house of the LORD.*

[6]*And I will add unto thy days fifteen years; and I will deliver thee and this city out of the hand of the king of*

Assyria; and I will defend this city for mine own sake, and for my servant David's sake.

Jabez sorrow; trouble

"Jabez, Oh that thou would bless me indeed"

I Chronicles 4:10

¹⁰ *And Jabez called on the God of Israel, saying, Oh that thou wouldest bless me indeed, and enlarge my coast, and that thine hand might be with me, and that thou wouldest keep me from evil, that it may not grieve me! And God granted him that which he requested.*

Reubenites the vision of the son

"The Reubenites pray for help and victory"

I Chronicles 5:18-22

[18] *The sons of Reuben, and the Gadites, and half the tribe of Manasseh, of valiant men, men able to bear buckler and sword, and to shoot with bow, and skilful in war, were four and forty thousand seven hundred and threescore, that went out to the war.*

[19] *And they made war with the Hagarites, with Jetur, and Nephish, and Nodab.*

[20] *And they were helped against them, and the Hagarites were delivered into their hand, and all that were with them: for they cried to God in the battle, and he was intreated of them; because they put their trust in him.*

[21] *And they took away their cattle; of their camels fifty thousand, and of sheep two hundred and fifty thousand, and of asses two thousand, and of men an hundred thousand.*

²²For there fell down many slain, because the war was of God. And they dwelt in their steads until the captivity.

Judah   the praise of Jehovah; confession

"And Judah gave a shout and cried unto the Lord "

II Chronicles 13:13-15

¹³But Jeroboam caused an ambushment to come about behind them: so they were before Judah, and the ambushment was behind them.

¹⁴And when Judah looked back, behold, the battle was before and behind: and they cried unto the LORD, and the priests sounded with the trumpets.

¹⁵Then the men of Judah gave a shout: and as the men of Judah shouted, it came to pass, that God smote Jeroboam and all Israel before Abijah and Judah.

"Oh Lord, thou art God, Let no man prevail against thee"

2 Chronicles 14:11-12

¹¹And Asa cried unto the LORD his God, and said, LORD, it is nothing with thee to help, whether with many, or with them that have no power: help us, O LORD our God; for we rest on thee, and in thy name we go against this multitude. O LORD, thou art our God; let no man prevail against thee.

¹²So the LORD smote the Ethiopians before Asa, and before Judah; and the Ethiopians fled.

Jehoshaphat **Jehovah is judge**

"Jehoshaphat cried out and the Lord helped him"

2 Chronicles 18:31

³¹And it came to pass, when the captains of the chariots saw Jehoshaphat, that they said, It is the king of Israel. Therefore they compassed about him to fight: but Jehoshaphat cried out, and the LORD helped him; and God moved them to depart from him.

"Judah Prayed O God our eyes are upon you"

II Chronicles 20:12-13 & 27

^{12}*O our God, wilt thou not judge them? for we have no might against this great company that cometh against us; neither know we what to do: but our eyes are upon thee.*

^{13}*And all Judah stood before the LORD, with their little ones, their wives, and their children.*

^{27}*Then they returned, every man of Judah and Jerusalem, and Jehoshaphat in the forefront of them, to go again to Jerusalem with joy; for the LORD had made them to rejoice over their enemies.*

Then the Priests the Levites arose and blessed the people

II Chronicles 30:27

^{27}*Then the priests the Levites arose and blessed the people: and their voice was heard, and their prayer came up to his holy dwelling place, even unto heaven.*

Manasseh *he that is forgotten*

"Then Manasseh knew that the Lord was his God"

II Chronicles 33:12-13

¹² And when he was in affliction, he besought the LORD his God, and humbled himself greatly before the God of his fathers,

¹³ And prayed unto him: and he was intreated of him, and heard his supplication, and brought him again to Jerusalem into his kingdom. Then Manasseh knew that the LORD he was God.

Ezra **help; court**

"Ezra proclaimed a fast to seek the Lord"

Ezra 8:21-23

²¹ Then I proclaimed a fast there, at the river of Ahava, that we might afflict ourselves before our God, to seek of him a right way for us, and for our little ones, and for all our substance.

²² For I was ashamed to require of the king a band of soldiers and horsemen to help us against the enemy in the way: because we had spoken unto the king, saying, The hand of our God is upon all them for good that seek him; but his power and his wrath is against all them that forsake him.

²³ So we fasted and besought our God for this: and he was intreated of us.

"Ezra fell upon his knees and prayed for the sins of the people"

Ezra 9:5-11

[5]*And at the evening sacrifice I arose up from my heaviness; and having rent my garment and my mantle, I fell upon my knees, and spread out my hands unto the LORD my God,*

[6]*And said, O my God, I am ashamed and blush to lift up my face to thee, my God: for our iniquities are increased over our head, and our trespass is grown up unto the heavens.*

[7]*Since the days of our fathers have we been in a great trespass unto this day; and for our iniquities have we, our kings, and our priests, been delivered into the hand of the kings of the lands, to the sword, to captivity, and to a spoil, and to confusion of face, as it is this day.*

[8]*And now for a little space grace hath been shewed from the LORD our God, to leave us a remnant to escape, and to give us a nail in his holy place, that our God may lighten our eyes, and give us a little reviving in our bondage.*

[9]*For we were bondmen; yet our God hath not forsaken us in our bondage, but hath extended mercy unto us in the sight of the kings of Persia, to give us a reviving, to set up the house of our God, and to repair the desolations thereof, and to give us a wall in Judah and in Jerusalem.*

[10]And now, O our God, what shall we say after this? for we have forsaken thy commandments,

[11]Which thou hast commanded by thy servants the prophets, saying, The land, unto which ye go to possess it, is an unclean land with the filthiness of the people of the lands, with their abominations, which have filled it from one end to another with their uncleanness.

Nehemiah   repentance of the Lord

"O Lord God of Heaven, the great and terrible God, be attentive to the prayer of thy Servant Nehemiah"

Nehemiah 1:3-11

[3]And they said unto me, The remnant that are left of the captivity there in the province are in great affliction and reproach: the wall of Jerusalem also is broken down, and the gates thereof are burned with fire.

[4]And it came to pass, when I heard these words, that I sat down and wept, and mourned certain days, and fasted, and prayed before the God of heaven,

⁵And said, I beseech thee, O LORD God of heaven, the great and terrible God, that keepeth covenant and mercy for them that love him and observe his commandments:

⁶Let thine ear now be attentive, and thine eyes open, that thou mayest hear the prayer of thy servant, which I pray before thee now, day and night, for the children of Israel thy servants, and confess the sins of the children of Israel, which we have sinned against thee: both I and my father's house have sinned.

⁷We have dealt very corruptly against thee, and have not kept the commandments, nor the statutes, nor the judgments, which thou commandedst thy servant Moses.

⁸Remember, I beseech thee, the word that thou commandedst thy servant Moses, saying, If ye transgress, I will scatter you abroad among the nations:

⁹But if ye turn unto me, and keep my commandments, and do them; though there were of you cast out unto the uttermost part of the heaven, yet will I gather them from thence, and will bring them unto the place that I have chosen to set my name there.

¹⁰Now these are thy servants and thy people, whom thou hast redeemed by thy great power, and by thy strong hand.

¹¹O LORD, I beseech thee, let now thine ear be attentive to the prayer of thy servant, and to the prayer of thy servants, who desire to fear thy name: and prosper, I pray thee, thy servant this day, and grant him mercy in the sight of this man. For I was the king's cupbearer.

Esther *secret; hidden*

"Esther's decree of fasting and prayer for her people"

Esther 4:3, 15-16

[3] *And in every province, whithersoever the king's commandment and his decree came, there was great mourning among the Jews, and fasting, and weeping, and wailing; and many lay in sackcloth and ashes.*

[15] *Then Esther bade them return Mordecai this answer,*

[16] *Go, gather together all the Jews that are present in Shushan, and fast ye for me, and neither eat nor drink three days, night or day: I also and my maidens will fast likewise; and so will I go in unto the king, which is not according to the law: and if I perish, I perish.*

Job **he that weeps or cries**

"Job's Sympathetic Prayer"

Job 1:20-21

[20] *Then Job arose, and rent his mantle, and shaved his head, and fell down upon the ground, and worshipped,*

[21] *And said, Naked came I out of my mother's womb, and naked shall I return thither: the LORD gave, and the LORD hath taken away; blessed be the name of the LORD.*

"Job's prayer for weariness of life"

Job 10:1-3, 18-19

[1] *My soul is weary of my life; I will leave my complaint upon myself; I will speak in the bitterness of my soul.*

[2] *I will say unto God, Do not condemn me; shew me wherefore thou contendest with me.*

³Is it good unto thee that thou shouldest oppress, that thou shouldest despise the work of thine hands, and shine upon the counsel of the wicked?

¹⁸Wherefore then hast thou brought me forth out of the womb? Oh that I had given up the ghost, and no eye had seen me!

¹⁹I should have been as though I had not been; I should have been carried from the womb to the grave.

"That which I see not"

Job 34:32

³²That which I see not teach thou me; if I have done iniquity I will do no more.

Prayer of the Psalms

Psalms 5:3

³My voice shalt thou hear in the morning, O LORD; in the morning will I direct my prayer unto thee, and will look up.

Psalms 17:1

[1]Hear the right, O LORD, attend unto my cry, give ear unto my prayer, that goeth not out of feigned lips.

Psalms 42:8

[8]Yet the LORD will command his lovingkindness in the day time, and in the night his song shall be with me, and my prayer unto the God of my life.

Psalms 51:1-19

[1]Have mercy upon me, O God, according to thy lovingkindness: according unto the multitude of thy tender mercies blot out my transgressions.

[2]Wash me throughly from mine iniquity, and cleanse me from my sin.

[3]For I acknowledge my transgressions: and my sin is ever before me.

[4]Against thee, thee only, have I sinned, and done this evil in thy sight: that thou mightest be justified when thou speakest, and be clear when thou judgest.

[5]Behold, I was shapen in iniquity; and in sin did my mother conceive me.

[6]Behold, thou desirest truth in the inward parts: and in the hidden part thou shalt make me to know wisdom.

[7]Purge me with hyssop, and I shall be clean: wash me, and I shall be whiter than snow.

[8]Make me to hear joy and gladness; that the bones which thou hast broken may rejoice.

[9]Hide thy face from my sins, and blot out all mine iniquities.

[10]Create in me a clean heart, O God; and renew a right spirit within me.

[11]Cast me not away from thy presence; and take not thy holy spirit from me.

[12]Restore unto me the joy of thy salvation; and uphold me with thy free spirit.

[13]Then will I teach transgressors thy ways; and sinners shall be converted unto thee.

[14]Deliver me from bloodguiltiness, O God, thou God of my salvation: and my tongue shall sing aloud of thy righteousness.

[15]O Lord, open thou my lips; and my mouth shall shew forth thy praise.

[16]For thou desirest not sacrifice; else would I give it: thou delightest not in burnt offering.

[17]The sacrifices of God are a broken spirit: a broken and a contrite heart, O God, thou wilt not despise.

¹⁸*Do good in thy good pleasure unto Zion: build thou the walls of Jerusalem.*

¹⁹*Then shalt thou be pleased with the sacrifices of righteousness, with burnt offering and whole burnt offering: then shall they offer bullocks upon thine altar.*

Psalms 54:2

²*Hear my prayer, O God; give ear to the words of my mouth.*

Psalms 61:1-3

¹*Hear my cry, O God; attend unto my prayer.*

²*From the end of the earth will I cry unto thee, when my heart is overwhelmed: lead me to the rock that is higher than I.*

³*For thou hast been a shelter for me, and a strong tower from the enemy.*

Psalms 65:2

²*O thou that hearest prayer, unto thee shall all flesh come.*

Psalms 66:19-20

¹⁹*But verily God hath heard me; he hath attended to the voice of my prayer.*

[20]Blessed be God, which hath not turned away my prayer, nor his mercy from me.

Psalms 69:13

[13]But as for me, my prayer is unto thee, O LORD, in an acceptable time: O God, in the multitude of thy mercy hear me, in the truth of thy salvation.

Psalms 86:6

[6]Give ear, O LORD, unto my prayer; and attend to the voice of my supplications.

Psalms 88:2 & 13

[2]Let my prayer come before thee: incline thine ear unto my cry;

[13]But unto thee have I cried, O LORD; and in the morning shall my prayer prevent thee.

Psalms 122:6

[6]Pray for the peace of Jerusalem: they shall prosper that love thee.

Psalms 143:1

[1]Hear my prayer, O LORD, give ear to my supplications: in thy faithfulness answer me, and in thy righteousness.

Isaiah **the salvation of the Lord**

"Woe is me! for I am undone"

Isaiah 6:1-7

¹ *In the year that king Uzziah died I saw also the LORD sitting upon a throne, high and lifted up, and his train filled the temple.*

² *Above it stood the seraphims: each one had six wings; with twain he covered his face, and with twain he covered his feet, and with twain he did fly.*

³ *And one cried unto another, and said, Holy, holy, holy, is the LORD of hosts: the whole earth is full of his glory.*

⁴ *And the posts of the door moved at the voice of him that cried, and the house was filled with smoke.*

⁵ *Then said I, Woe is me! for I am undone; because I am a man of unclean lips, and I dwell in the midst of a people of unclean lips: for mine eyes have seen the King, the LORD of hosts.*

⁶Then flew one of the seraphims unto me, having a live coal in his hand, which he had taken with the tongs from off the altar:

⁷And he laid it upon my mouth, and said, Lo, this hath touched thy lips; and thine iniquity is taken away, and thy sin purged.

"Joyful in the House of Prayer"

Isaiah 56:7

⁷Even them will I bring to my holy mountain, and make them joyful in my house of prayer: their burnt offerings and their sacrifices shall be accepted upon mine altar; for mine house shall be called an house of prayer for all people.

Jeremiah   **exaltation of Jehovah**

"My eyes a fountain of tears"

Jeremiah 9:1; 17&18

¹Oh that my head were waters, and mine eyes a fountain of tears, that I might weep day and night for the slain of the daughter of my people!

¹⁷*Thus saith the Lord of hosts, Consider ye, and call for the mourning women, that they may come: and send for cunning women, that they may come:*

¹⁸*And let them make haste, and take up a wailing for us, that our eyelids gush out with waters.*

"Call upon me"

Jeremiah 29:12

¹²*Then shall ye call upon me, and ye shall go and pray unto me, and I will hearken unto you.*

"Jeremiah prays, Lord, Show us the way wherein we may walk"

Jeremiah 42:1-6

¹*Then all the captains of the forces, and Johanan the son of Kareah, and Jezaniah the son of Hoshaiah, and all the people from the least even unto the greatest, came near,*

²*And said unto Jeremiah the prophet, Let, we beseech thee, our supplication be accepted before thee, and pray for us unto the LORD thy God, even for all this remnant; (for we are left but a few of many, as thine eyes do behold us:)*

³*That the LORD thy God may shew us the way wherein we may walk, and the thing that we may do.*

⁴*Then Jeremiah the prophet said unto them, I have heard you; behold, I will pray unto the LORD your God*

89

according to your words; and it shall come to pass, that whatsoever thing the LORD shall answer you, I will declare it unto you; I will keep nothing back from you.

[5] Then they said to Jeremiah, The LORD be a true and faithful witness between us, if we do not even according to all things for the which the LORD thy God shall send thee to us.

[6] Whether it be good, or whether it be evil, we will obey the voice of the LORD our God, to whom we send thee; that it may be well with us, when we obey the voice of the LORD our God.

Ezekial

the strength of God, God strengthens

"Ezekiel prays, Ah Lord God! behold, my soul hath not been polluted"

Ezekiel 4:12-15

[12] And thou shalt eat it as barley cakes, and thou shalt bake it with dung that cometh out of man, in their sight.

[13] And the LORD said, Even thus shall the children of Israel eat their defiled bread among the Gentiles, whither I will drive them.

[14]*Then said I, Ah Lord GOD! behold, my soul hath not been polluted: for from my youth up even till now have I not eaten of that which dieth of itself, or is torn in pieces; neither came there abominable flesh into my mouth.*

[15]*Then he said unto me, Lo, I have given thee cow's dung for man's dung, and thou shalt prepare thy bread therewith.*

"Thou knowest"

Ezekiel 37:1-5

[1]*The hand of the Lord was upon me, and carried me out in the spirit of the Lord, and set me down in the midst of the valley which was full of bones,*

[2]*And caused me to pass by them round about: and, behold there were very many in the open valley; and, lo, they were very dry.*

[3]*And he said unto me, Son of man, can these bones live? And I answered, O Lord God, thou knowest.*

[4]*Again he said unto me, Prophesy upon these bones, and say unto them, I ye dry bones, hear they word of the Lord.*

[5]*Thus saith the Lord God unto these bones; Behold, I will cause breath to enter into you, and ye shall live:*

Daniel judgment of God; God my judge

"Wisdom and Might are his"
Daniel 2:19-23

¹⁹*Then was the secret revealed unto Daniel in a night vision. Then Daniel blessed the God of heaven.*

²⁰*Daniel answered and said, Blessed be the name of God for ever and ever: for wisdom and might are his:*

²¹*And he changeth the times and the seasons: he removeth kings, and setteth up kings: he giveth wisdom unto the wise, and knowledge to them that know understanding:*

²²*He revealeth the deep and secret things: he knoweth what is in the darkness, and the light dwelleth with him.*

²³*I thank thee, and praise thee, O thou God of my fathers, who hast given me wisdom and might, and hast made known unto me now what we desired of thee: for thou hast now made known unto us the king's matter.*

"He kneeled and prayed three times a day"
Daniel 6:10-11

[10]Now when Daniel knew that the writing was signed, he went into his house; and his windows being open in his chamber toward Jerusalem, he kneeled upon his knees three times a day, and prayed, and gave thanks before his God, as he did aforetime.

[11]Then these men assembled, and found Daniel praying and making supplication before his God.

"I set my face to seek God"
Daniel 9:3-4 & 17

[3]And I set my face unto the Lord God, to seek by prayer and supplications, with fasting, and sackcloth, and ashes:

[4]And I prayed unto the LORD my God, and made my confession, and said, O Lord, the great and dreadful God, keeping the covenant and mercy to them that love him, and to them that keep his commandments;

[17]Now therefore, O our God, hear the prayer of thy servant, and his supplications, and cause thy face to shine upon thy sanctuary that is desolate, for the Lord's sake.

93

Jonah **a dove; he that oppresses; destroyer**

"Jonah's prayer, they that observe lying vanities"
Jonah 2:1-10

1 Then Jonah prayed unto the LORD his God out of the fish's belly,

2 And said, I cried by reason of mine affliction unto the LORD, and he heard me; out of the belly of hell cried I, and thou heardest my voice.

3 For thou hadst cast me into the deep, in the midst of the seas; and the floods compassed me about: all thy billows and thy waves passed over me.

4 Then I said, I am cast out of thy sight; yet I will look again toward thy holy temple.

5 The waters compassed me about, even to the soul: the depth closed me round about, the weeds were wrapped about my head.

6 I went down to the bottoms of the mountains; the earth with her bars was about me for ever: yet hast thou brought up my life from corruption, O LORD my God.

[7]*When my soul fainted within me I remembered the LORD: and my prayer came in unto thee, into thine holy temple.*

[8]*They that observe lying vanities forsake their own mercy.*

[9]*But I will sacrifice unto thee with the voice of thanksgiving; I will pay that that I have vowed. Salvation is of the LORD.*

[10]*And the LORD spake unto the fish, and it vomited out Jonah upon the dry land.*

Jonah's anger at the Lord's compassion, the Prayer
Jonah 4:1-4

[1]*But it displeased Jonah exceedingly, and he was very angry.*

[2]*And he prayed unto the LORD, and said, I pray thee, O LORD, was not this my saying, when I was yet in my country? Therefore I fled before unto Tarshish: for I knew that thou art a gracious God, and merciful, slow to anger, and of great kindness, and repentest thee of the evil.*

[3]*Therefore now, O LORD, take, I beseech thee, my life from me; for it is better for me to die than to live.*

[4]*Then said the LORD, Doest thou well to be angry?*

Habakkuk

he that embraces; a wrestler

"Habakkuk's prayer, Oh Lord how long shall I cry"
Habakkuk's 1:1-7

1 The burden which Habakkuk the prophet did see.

2 O LORD, how long shall I cry, and thou wilt not hear! even cry out unto thee of violence, and thou wilt not save!

3 Why dost thou shew me iniquity, and cause me to behold grievance? for spoiling and violence are before me: and there are that raise up strife and contention.

4 Therefore the law is slacked, and judgment doth never go forth: for the wicked doth compass about the righteous; therefore wrong judgment proceedeth.

5 Behold ye among the heathen, and regard, and wonder marvelously: for I will work a work in your days which ye will not believe, though it be told you.

6 For, lo, I raise up the Chaldeans, that bitter and hasty nation, which shall march through the breadth of the land, to possess the dwellingplaces that are not their's.

[7]They are terrible and dreadful: their judgment and their dignity shall proceed of themselves.

"Remember Mercy"

Habakkuk 3:1-2

[1]A prayer of Habakkuk the prophet upon Shigionoth.

[2]O LORD, I have heard thy speech, and was afraid: O LORD, revive thy work in the midst of the years, in the midst of the years make known; in wrath remember mercy.

New Testament

Matthew 6:9-15

⁹ *After this manner therefore pray ye: Our Father which art in heaven, Hallowed be thy name.*

¹⁰ *Thy kingdom come, Thy will be done in earth, as it is in heaven.*

¹¹ *Give us this day our daily bread.*

¹² *And forgive us our debts, as we forgive our debtors.*

¹³ *And lead us not into temptation, but deliver us from evil: For thine is the kingdom, and the power, and the glory, for ever. Amen.*

¹⁴ *For if ye forgive men their trespasses, your heavenly Father will also forgive you:*

¹⁵ *But if ye forgive not men their trespasses, neither will your Father forgive your trespasses.*

Jesus Jehovah is salvation; deliverer; help

"Prayer on a Mountain"

Matthew 14:23

²³ *And when he had sent the multitudes away, he went up into a mountain apart to pray: and when the evening was come, he was there alone.*

"Gethsemane, Let this cup pass from me"

Matthew 26:39-42

³⁹ *And he went a little farther, and fell on his face, and prayed, saying, O my Father, if it be possible, let this cup pass from me: nevertheless not as I will, but as thou wilt.*

⁴⁰ *And he cometh unto the disciples, and findeth them asleep, and saith unto Peter, What, could ye not watch with me one hour?*

⁴¹ *Watch and pray, that ye enter not into temptation: the spirit indeed is willing, but the flesh is weak.*

[42]*He went away again the second time, and prayed, saying, O my Father, if this cup may not pass away.*

"Eli Eli Lama Sabachthani?"

Matthew 27:46

[46]*And about the ninth hour Jesus cried with a loud voice, saying, Eli, Eli, lama sabachthani? that is to say, My God, my God, why hast thou forsaken me?*

"Praying early in the morning"

Mark 1:35

[35]*And in the morning, rising up a great while before day, he went out, and departed into a solitary place, and there prayed.*

Mark 15:34

[34]*And at the ninth hour Jesus cried with a loud voice, saying, Eloi, Eloi, lama sabachthani? which is, being interpreted, My God, my God, why hast thou forsaken me?*

"Men ought to always Pray"

Luke 18:1

[1]*And he spake a parable unto them to this end, that men ought always to pray, and not to faint*

Luke 23:34

34 Then said Jesus, Father, forgive them; for they know not what they do. And they parted his raiment, and cast lots.

"Lord, Remember Me "

Luke 23:40-45

40 But the other answering rebuked him, saying, Dost not thou fear God, seeing thou art in the same condemnation?

41 And we indeed justly; for we receive the due reward of our deeds: but this man hath done nothing amiss.

42 And he said unto Jesus, Lord, remember me when thou comest into thy kingdom.

43 And Jesus said unto him, Verily I say unto thee, Today shalt thou be with me in paradise.

44 And it was about the sixth hour, and there was a darkness over all the earth until the ninth hour.

45 And the sun was darkened, and the veil of the temple was rent in the midst.

"*Father, into thy hands I commend my Spirit*"

Luke 23:46

⁴⁶And when Jesus had cried with a loud voice, he said, Father, into thy hands I commend my spirit: and having said thus, he gave up the ghost.

Prayer of Jesus for His Church

"*Jesus Prays, Glorify thy Son*"

John 17:1-4

¹These words spake Jesus, and lifted up his eyes to heaven, and said, Father, the hour is come; glorify thy Son, that thy Son also may glorify thee:

²As thou hast given him power over all flesh, that he should give eternal life to as many as thou hast given him.

³And this is life eternal, that they might know thee the only true God, and Jesus Christ, whom thou hast sent.

⁴I have glorified thee on the earth: I have finished the work which thou gavest me to do.

"Jesus Prays for His Disciples, Sanctify them through thy truth"

[6]I have manifested thy name unto the men which thou gavest me out of the world: thine they were, and thou gavest them me; and they have kept thy word.

[7]Now they have known that all things whatsoever thou hast given me are of thee.

[8]For I have given unto them the words which thou gavest me; and they have received them, and have known surely that I came out from thee, and they have believed that thou didst send me.

[9]I pray for them: I pray not for the world, but for them which thou hast given me; for they are thine.

[10]And all mine are thine, and thine are mine; and I am glorified in them.

[11]And now I am no more in the world, but these are in the world, and I come to thee. Holy Father, keep through thine own name those whom thou hast given me, that they may be one, as we are.

[12]While I was with them in the world, I kept them in thy name: those that thou gavest me I have kept, and none of them is lost, but the son of perdition; that the scripture might be fulfilled.

[13]*And now come I to thee; and these things I speak in the world, that they might have my joy fulfilled in themselves.*

[14]*I have given them thy word; and the world hath hated them, because they are not of the world, even as I am not of the world.*

[15]*I pray not that thou shouldest take them out of the world, but that thou shouldest keep them from the evil.*

[16]*They are not of the world, even as I am not of the world.*

[17]*Sanctify them through thy truth: thy word is truth.*

[18]*As thou hast sent me into the world, even so have I also sent them into the world.*

[19]*And for their sakes I sanctify myself, that they also might be sanctified through the truth.*

"*Jesus prays for all believers, that they be One*"

John 17:20-26

[20]*Neither pray I for these alone, but for them also which shall believe on me through their word;*

[21]*That they all may be one; as thou, Father, art in me, and I in thee, that they also may be one in us: that the world may believe that thou hast sent me.*

²²*And the glory which thou gavest me I have given them; that they may be one, even as we are one:*

²³*I in them, and thou in me, that they may be made perfect in one; and that the world may know that thou hast sent me, and hast loved them, as thou hast loved me.*

²⁴*Father, I will that they also, whom thou hast given me, be with me where I am; that they may behold my glory, which thou hast given me: for thou lovedst me before the foundation of the world.*

²⁵*O righteous Father, the world hath not known thee: but I have known thee, and these have known that thou hast sent me.*

²⁶*And I have declared unto them thy name, and will declare it: that the love wherewith thou hast loved me may be in them, and I in them.*

"Woman, Behold thy Son"

John 19:26-27

²⁶*When Jesus therefore saw his mother, and the disciple standing by, whom he loved, he saith unto his mother, Woman, behold thy son!*

²⁷*Then saith he to the disciple, Behold thy mother! And from that hour that disciple took her unto his own home.*

"If thou wouldest believe"

John 11:40-43

⁴⁰Jesus saith unto her, Said I not unto thee, that, if thou wouldest believe, thou shouldest see the glory of God?

⁴¹Then they took away the stone from the place where the dead was laid. And Jesus lifted up his eyes, and said, Father, I thank thee that thou hast heard me.

⁴²And I knew that thou hearest me always: but because of the people which stand by I said it, that they may believe that thou hast sent me.

⁴³And when he thus had spoken, he cried with a loud voice, Lazarus, come forth.

"Father Glorify thy Name"

John 12:28

²⁸Father, glorify thy name. Then came there a voice from heaven, saying, I have both glorified it, and will glorify it again.

Prayer of the Centurion

"Lord, My Servant lieth at home sick"

Matthew 8:5-9; 13

⁵ *And when Jesus was entered into Capernaum, there came unto him a centurion, beseeching him,*

⁶ *And saying, Lord, my servant lieth at home sick of the palsy, grievously tormented.*

⁷ *And Jesus saith unto him, I will come and heal him.*

⁸ *The centurion answered and said, Lord, I am not worthy that thou shouldest come under my roof: but speak the word only, and my servant shall be healed.*

⁹ *For I am a man under authority, having soldiers under me: and I say to this man, Go, and he goeth; and to another, Come, and he cometh; and to my servant, Do this, and he doeth it.*

¹³ *And Jesus said unto the centurion, Go thy way; and as thou hast believed, so be it done unto thee. And his servant was healed in the selfsame hour.*

Prayer of the Leper

"If thou wilt, make me clean"

Mark 1:40-44

[40] *And there came a leper to him, beseeching him, and kneeling down to him, and saying unto him, If thou wilt, thou canst make me clean.*

[41] *And Jesus, moved with compassion, put forth his hand, and touched him, and saith unto him, I will; be thou clean.*

[42] *And as soon as he had spoken, immediately the leprosy departed from him, and he was cleansed.*

[43] *And he straitly charged him, and forthwith sent him away;*

[44] *And saith unto him, See thou say nothing to any man: but go thy way, shew thyself to the priest, and offer for thy cleansing those things which Moses commanded, for a testimony unto them.*

Prayer of Blind Bartimaeus

"Thou Son of David, Have Mercy"

Mark 10:46-52

⁴⁶ And they came to Jericho: and as he went out of Jericho with his disciples and a great number of people, blind Bartimaeus, the son of Timaeus, sat by the highway side begging.

⁴⁷ And when he heard that it was Jesus of Nazareth, he began to cry out, and say, Jesus, thou son of David, have mercy on me.

⁴⁸ And many charged him that he should hold his peace: but he cried the more a great deal, Thou son of David, have mercy on me.

⁴⁹ And Jesus stood still, and commanded him to be called. And they call the blind man, saying unto him, Be of good comfort, rise; he calleth thee.

⁵⁰ And he, casting away his garment, rose, and came to Jesus.

⁵¹*And Jesus answered and said unto him, What wilt thou that I should do unto thee? The blind man said unto him, Lord, that I might receive my sight.*

⁵²*And Jesus said unto him, Go thy way; thy faith hath made thee whole. And immediately he received his sight, and followed Jesus in the way.*

Zechariah *remembered by the Lord*

"Zechariah Prays for his wife to bear a son"

Luke 1:13

¹³*But the angel said unto him, Fear not, Zacharias: for thy prayer is heard; and thy wife Elisabeth shall bear thee a son, and thou shalt call his name John.*

Stephen **crown; crowned**

"Prayer of Stephen"

Acts 7:59-60

[59] *And they stoned Stephen, calling upon God, and saying, Lord Jesus, receive my spirit.*

[60] *And he kneeled down, and cried with a loud voice, Lord, lay not this sin to their charge. And when he had said this, he fell asleep.*

Peter **a rock or stone**

"Bid me Come"

Matthew 14:28-30

[28] *And Peter answered him and said, Lord, if it be thou, bid me come unto thee on the water.*

112

[29]And he said, Come. And when Peter was come down out of the ship, he walked on the water, to go to Jesus.

[30]But when he saw the wind boisterous, he was afraid; and beginning to sink, he cried, saying, Lord, save me.

"Pentecost came after 9 days of prayer"

Acts 1:12-14

[12]Then returned they unto Jerusalem from the mount called Olivet, which is from Jerusalem a sabbath day's journey.

[13]And when they were come in, they went up into an upper room, where abode both Peter, and James, and John, and Andrew, Philip, and Thomas, Bartholomew, and Matthew, James the son of Alphaeus, and Simon Zelotes, and Judas the brother of James.

[14]These all continued with one accord in prayer and supplication, with the women, and Mary the mother of Jesus, and with his brethren.

"Peter prayed and said "Tabitha Arise""

Acts 9:36-40

[36]Now there was at Joppa a certain disciple named Tabitha, which by interpretation is called Dorcas: this woman was full of good works and almsdeeds which she did.

³⁷And it came to pass in those days, that she was sick, and died: whom when they had washed, they laid her in an upper chamber.

³⁸And forasmuch as Lydda was nigh to Joppa, and the disciples had heard that Peter was there, they sent unto him two men, desiring him that he would not delay to come to them.

³⁹Then Peter arose and went with them. When he was come, they brought him into the upper chamber: and all the widows stood by him weeping, and shewing the coats and garments which Dorcas made, while she was with them.

⁴⁰But Peter put them all forth, and kneeled down, and prayed; and turning him to the body said, Tabitha, arise. And she opened her eyes: and when she saw Peter, she sat up.

Paul **small; little**

"Paul prays for the Romans"

Romans 1:7-9

⁷*To all that be in Rome, beloved of God, called to be saints: Grace to you and peace from God our Father, and the Lord Jesus Christ.*

⁸*First, I thank my God through Jesus Christ for you all, that your faith is spoken of throughout the whole world.*

⁹*For God is my witness, whom I serve with my spirit in the gospel of his Son, that without ceasing I make mention of you always in my prayers.*

"He helpeth our infirmities"

Romans 8:26

²⁶*Likewise the Spirit also helpeth our infirmities: for we know not what we should pray for as we ought: but the Spirit itself maketh intercession for us with groanings which cannot be uttered.*

115

"Paul prays for Salvation of Israel"

Romans 10:1

[1]*Brethren, my heart's desire and prayer to God for Israel is, that they might be saved.*

"That you be refreshed"

Romans 15:30-33

[30]*Now I beseech you, brethren, for the Lord Jesus Christ's sake, and for the love of the Spirit, that ye strive together with me in your prayers to God for me;*

[31]*That I may be delivered from them that do not believe in Judaea; and that my service which I have for Jerusalem may be accepted of the saints;*

[32]*That I may come unto you with joy by the will of God, and may with you be refreshed.*

[33]*Now the God of peace be with you all. Amen.*

"Paul & Silas"

Acts 16:25

[25]*And at midnight Paul and Silas prayed, and sang praises unto God: and the prisoners heard them.*

Paul prays for the father of Publius

Acts 28:7-10

⁷*In the same quarters were possessions of the chief man of the island, whose name was Publius; who received us, and lodged us three days courteously.*

⁸*And it came to pass, that the father of Publius lay sick of a fever and of a bloody flux: to whom Paul entered in, and prayed, and laid his hands on him, and healed him.*

⁹*So when this was done, others also, which had diseases in the island, came, and were healed:*

¹⁰*Who also honoured us with many honours; and when we departed, they laded us with such things as were necessary.*

Prayer for the Church at Corinth

"Prayer of Thanksgiving"

I Corinthians 11:23-26

²³*For I have received of the Lord that which also I delivered unto you, that the Lord Jesus the same night in which he was betrayed took bread:*

^{24}*And when he had given thanks, he brake it, and said, Take, eat: this is my body, which is broken for you: this do in remembrance of me.*

^{25}*After the same manner also he took the cup, when he had supped, saying, this cup is the new testament in my blood: this do ye, as oft as ye drink it, in remembrance of me.*

^{26}*For as often as ye eat this bread, and drink this cup, ye do shew the Lord's death till he come.*

"Praying in the Spirit"

I Corinthians 12:3

^{3}*Wherefore I give you to understand, that no man speaking by the Spirit of God calleth Jesus accursed: and that no man can say that Jesus is the Lord, but by the Holy Ghost.*

"Paul prays for grace, the thorn in the flesh"

II Corinthians 12:8-10

^{8}*For this thing I besought the Lord thrice, that it might depart from me.*

^{9}*And he said unto me, My grace is sufficient for thee: for my strength is made perfect in weakness. Most gladly therefore will I rather glory in my infirmities, that the power of Christ may rest upon me.*

^{10}*Therefore I take pleasure in infirmities, in reproaches, in necessities, in persecutions, in distresses for Christ's sake: for when I am weak, then am I strong.*

"Prayer to Jesus, the Father and the Spirit"

II Corinthians 13:4

^{4}*For though he was crucified through weakness, yet he liveth by the power of God. For we also are weak in him, but we shall live with him by the power of God toward you.*

"Do that which is honest"

II Corinthians 13:7

^{7}*Now I pray to God that ye do no evil; not that we should appear approved, but that ye should do that which is honest, though we be as reprobates.*

Prayers for the Ephesians

"Thanksgiving and Payer of Paul"

Ephesians 1:15-22

^{15}*Wherefore I also, after I heard of your faith in the Lord Jesus, and love unto all the saints,*

¹⁶Cease not to give thanks for you, making mention of you in my prayers;

¹⁷That the God of our Lord Jesus Christ, the Father of glory, may give unto you the spirit of wisdom and revelation in the knowledge of him:

¹⁸The eyes of your understanding being enlightened; that ye may know what is the hope of his calling, and what the riches of the glory of his inheritance in the saints,

¹⁹And what is the exceeding greatness of his power to us-ward who believe, according to the working of his mighty power,

²⁰Which he wrought in Christ, when he raised him from the dead, and set him at his own right hand in the heavenly places,

²¹Far above all principality, and power, and might, and dominion, and every name that is named, not only in this world, but also in that which is to come:

²²And hath put all things under his feet, and gave him to be the head over all things to the church,

"That ye be rooted and grounded in Love"

Ephesians 3:14-21

^{14}*For this cause I bow my knees unto the Father of our Lord Jesus Christ,*

^{15}*Of whom the whole family in heaven and earth is named,*

^{16}*That he would grant you, according to the riches of his glory, to be strengthened with might by his Spirit in the inner man;*

^{17}*That Christ may dwell in your hearts by faith; that ye, being rooted and grounded in love,*

^{18}*May be able to comprehend with all saints what is the breadth, and length, and depth, and height;*

^{19}*And to know the love of Christ, which passeth knowledge, that ye might be filled with all the fulness of God.*

^{20}*Now unto him that is able to do exceeding abundantly above all that we ask or think, according to the power that worketh in us,*

^{21}*Unto him be glory in the church by Christ Jesus throughout all ages, world without end. Amen.*

Ephesians 6:18-19

[18]*Praying always with all prayer and supplication in the Spirit, and watching thereunto with all perseverance and supplication for all saints;*

[19]*And for me, that utterance may be given unto me, that I may open my mouth boldly, to make known the mystery of the gospel.*

Prayer for the Church at Philippi

"Prayer for Abounding Love"

Philippians 1:9-11

[9]*And this I pray, that your love may abound yet more and more in knowledge and in all judgment;*

[10]*That ye may approve things that are excellent; that ye may be sincere and without offence till the day of Christ.*

[11]*Being filled with the fruits of righteousness, which are by Jesus Christ, unto the glory and praise of God.*

"Let your requests be made known"

Philippians 4:6

⁶Be careful for nothing; but in every thing by prayer and supplication with thanksgiving let your requests be made known unto God.

Prayer for the Colossians

"Praying always for You"

Colossians 1:3-4

³We give thanks to God and the Father of our Lord Jesus Christ, praying always for you,

⁴Since we heard of your faith in Christ Jesus, and of the love which ye have to all the saints,

"Knowledge, wisdom and understanding, Paul's Prayer"

Colossians 1:9

⁹For this cause we also, since the day we heard it, do not cease to pray for you, and to desire that ye might be filled with the knowledge of his will in all wisdom and spiritual understanding;

123

"Continue in Prayer and Watch"

Colossians 4:2-4

²Continue in prayer, and watch in the same with thanksgiving;

³Withal praying also for us, that God would open unto us a door of utterance, to speak the mystery of Christ, for which I am also in bonds:

⁴That I may make it manifest, as I ought to speak.

Prayer for the Thessalonians

"That ye walk Worthy"

2 Thessalonians 1:11-12

¹¹Wherefore also we pray always for you, that our God would count you worthy of this calling, and fulfil all the good pleasure of his goodness, and the work of faith with power:

¹²That the name of our Lord Jesus Christ may be glorified in you, and ye in him, according to the grace of our God and the Lord Jesus Christ.

"Pray for us, that the Word will have free course"

2 Thessalonians 3:1

¹*Finally, brethren, pray for us, that the word of the Lord may have free course, and be glorified, even as it is with you:*

Timothy revere God

"Christians' prayers for Kings in Authority"

I Timothy 2:1-2

¹*I exhort therefore, that, first of all, supplications, prayers, intercessions, and giving of thanks, be made for all men;*

²*For kings, and for all that are in authority; that we may lead a quiet and peaceable life in all godliness and honesty.*

II Timothy 1:3-4

³*I thank God, whom I serve from my forefathers with pure conscience, that without ceasing I have remembrance of thee in my prayers night and day;*

4Greatly desiring to see thee, being mindful of thy tears, that I may be filled with joy;

Philemon, loving

"Prayer of Thanksgiving"

Philemon 1:4-6

⁴*I thank my God, making mention of thee always in my prayers,*

⁵*Hearing of thy love and faith, which thou hast toward the Lord Jesus, and toward all saints;*

⁶*That the communication of thy faith may become effectual by the acknowledging of every good thing which is in you in Christ Jesus.*

"Pray for us"

Hebrews 13:18-19

^{18}*P*ray for us: for we trust we have a good conscience, in all things willing to live honestly.

^{19}*But I beseech you the rather to do this, that I may be restored to you the sooner.*

"Prayer to the God of Peace "

Hebrews 13:20-21

^{20}*Now the God of peace, that brought again from the dead our Lord Jesus, that great shepherd of the sheep, through the blood of the everlasting covenant,*

^{21}*Make you perfect in every good work to do his will, working in you that which is wellpleasing in his sight, through Jesus Christ; to whom be glory for ever and ever. Amen.*

James   **a form of Jacob**

"The Effectual Fervent Prayer"

James 5:13-16

[13] *Is any among you afflicted? let him pray. Is any merry? let him sing psalms.*

[14] *Is any sick among you? let him call for the elders of the church; and let them pray over him, anointing him with oil in the name of the Lord:*

[15] *And the prayer of faith shall save the sick, and the Lord shall raise him up; and if he have committed sins, they shall be forgiven him.*

[16] *Confess your faults one to another, and pray one for another, that ye may be healed. The effectual fervent prayer of a righteous man availeth much.*

1 & 3 John

"Prayer of Petition"

I John 5:14-15

^{14}*And this is the confidence that we have in him, that, if we ask any thing according to his will, he heareth us:*

^{15}*And if we know that he hear us, whatsoever we ask, we know that we have the petitions that we desired of him.*

"That thou mayest prosper"

3 John 1:2-4

^{2}*Beloved, I wish above all things that thou mayest prosper and be in health, even as thy soul prospereth.*

^{3}*For I rejoiced greatly, when the brethren came and testified of the truth that is in thee, even as thou walkest in the truth.*

^{4}*I have no greater joy than to hear that my children walk in truth.*

Revelation revealed

"Prayer of the Saints"

Revelation 5:8

[8] *And when he had taken the book, the four beasts and four and twenty elders fell down before the Lamb, having every one of them harps, and golden vials full of odours, which are the prayers of saints.*

Revelation 8:3-4

[3] *And another angel came and stood at the altar, having a golden censer; and there was given unto him much incense, that he should offer it with the prayers of all saints upon the golden altar which was before the throne.*

[4] *And the smoke of the incense, which came with the prayers of the saints, ascended up before God out of the angel's hand.*

To obtain your copy of the publications
"Let Us Pray Together Now" *or*
"War In The Spirit and Win",
Written by Dr. Angie Ray,
visit our online Bookstore,
www.angierayministries.com.

For more information:

Pastor Kimberly Ray
Angie Ray Ministries
P.O. Box 1104
Matteson, Illinois 60443
www.kimberlyrayministries.com

Angie Ray Ministries
"Church On The Rock"
4013 Lindenwood Drive
Matteson, IL 60443